I0454632

This coloringbook belongs to:

Published by: Matt Bowman
Cover and Illustrations by Matt Bowman
AI generators were used in the design of images.
First Printing: 12/23

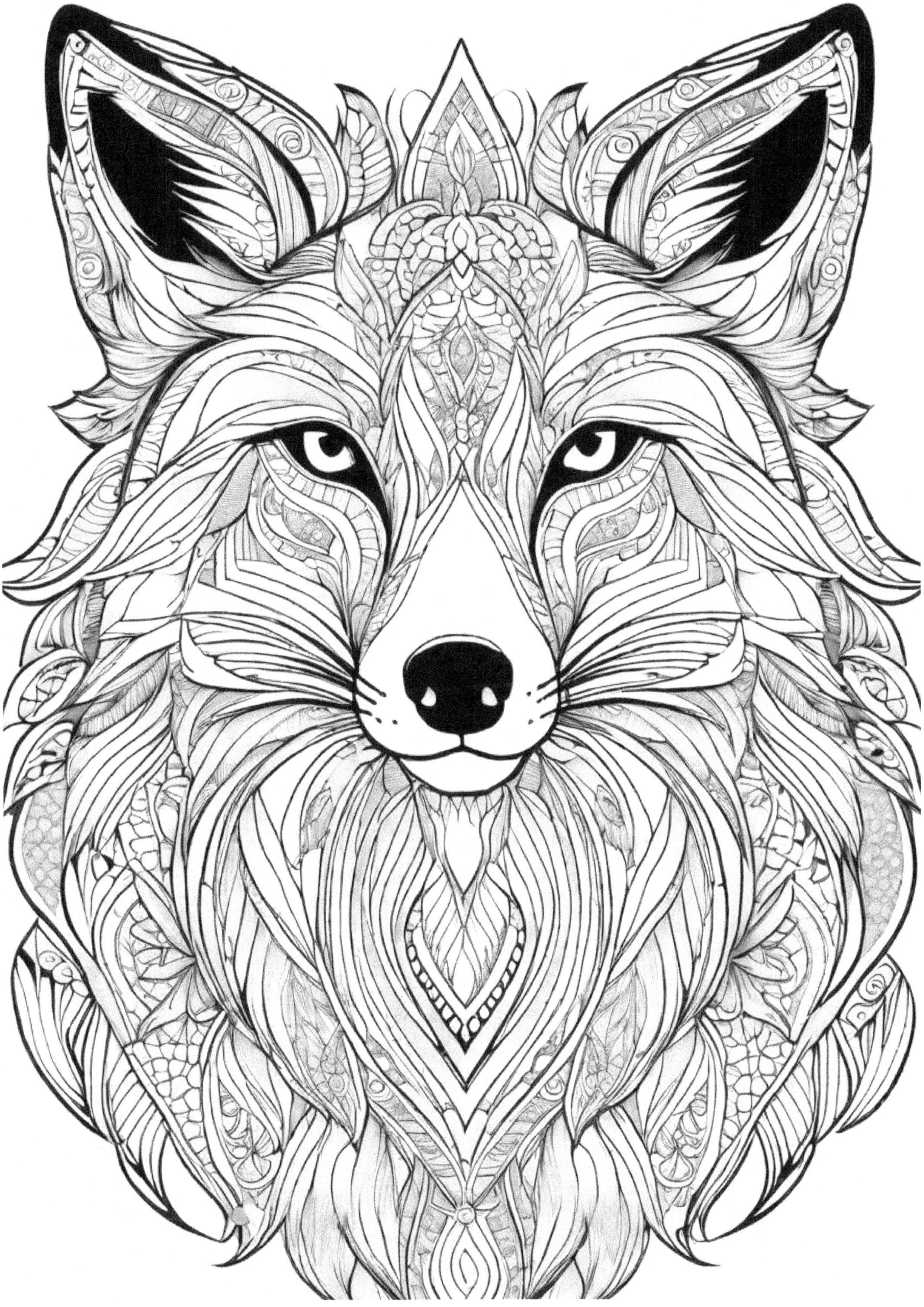

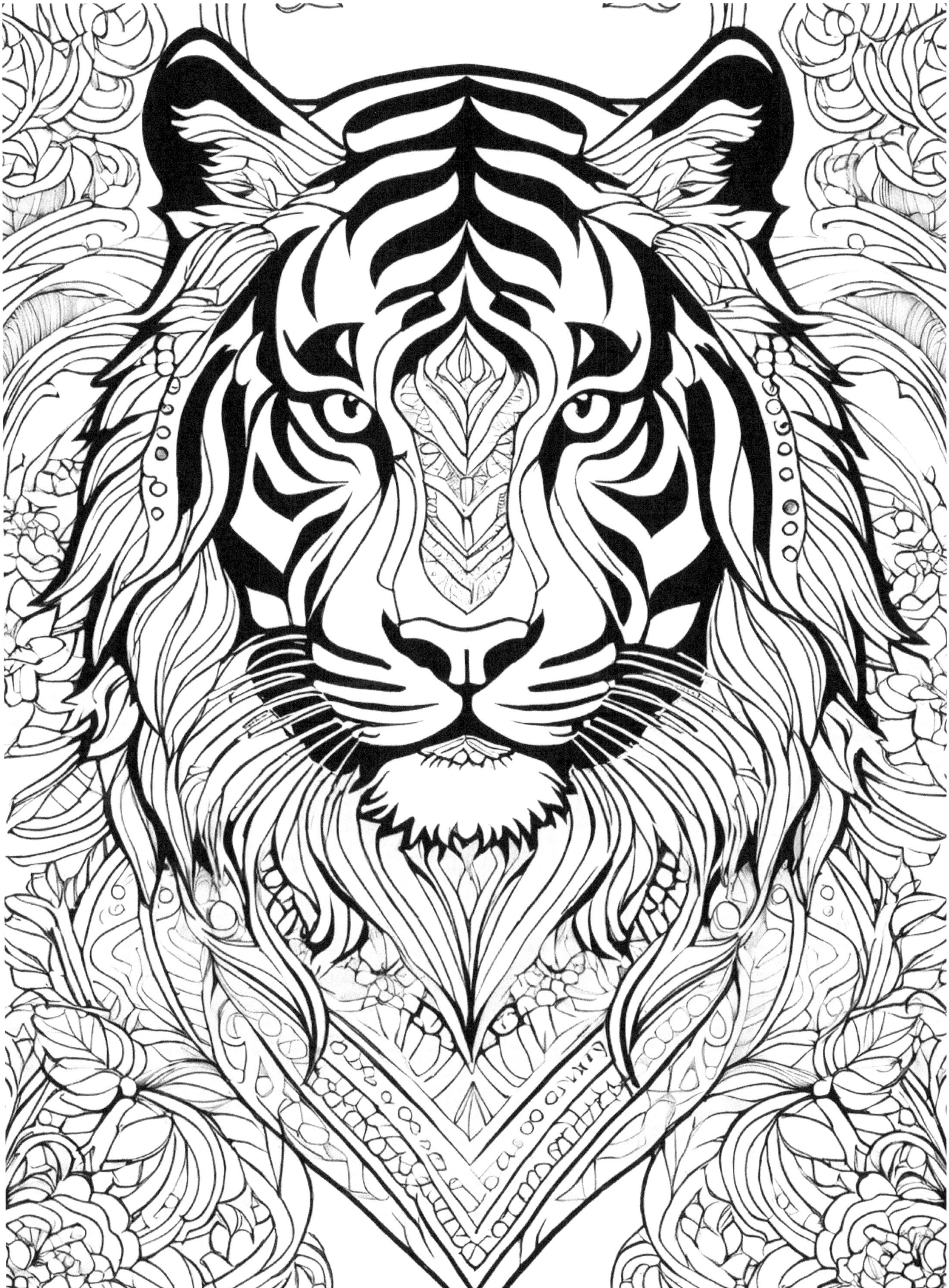

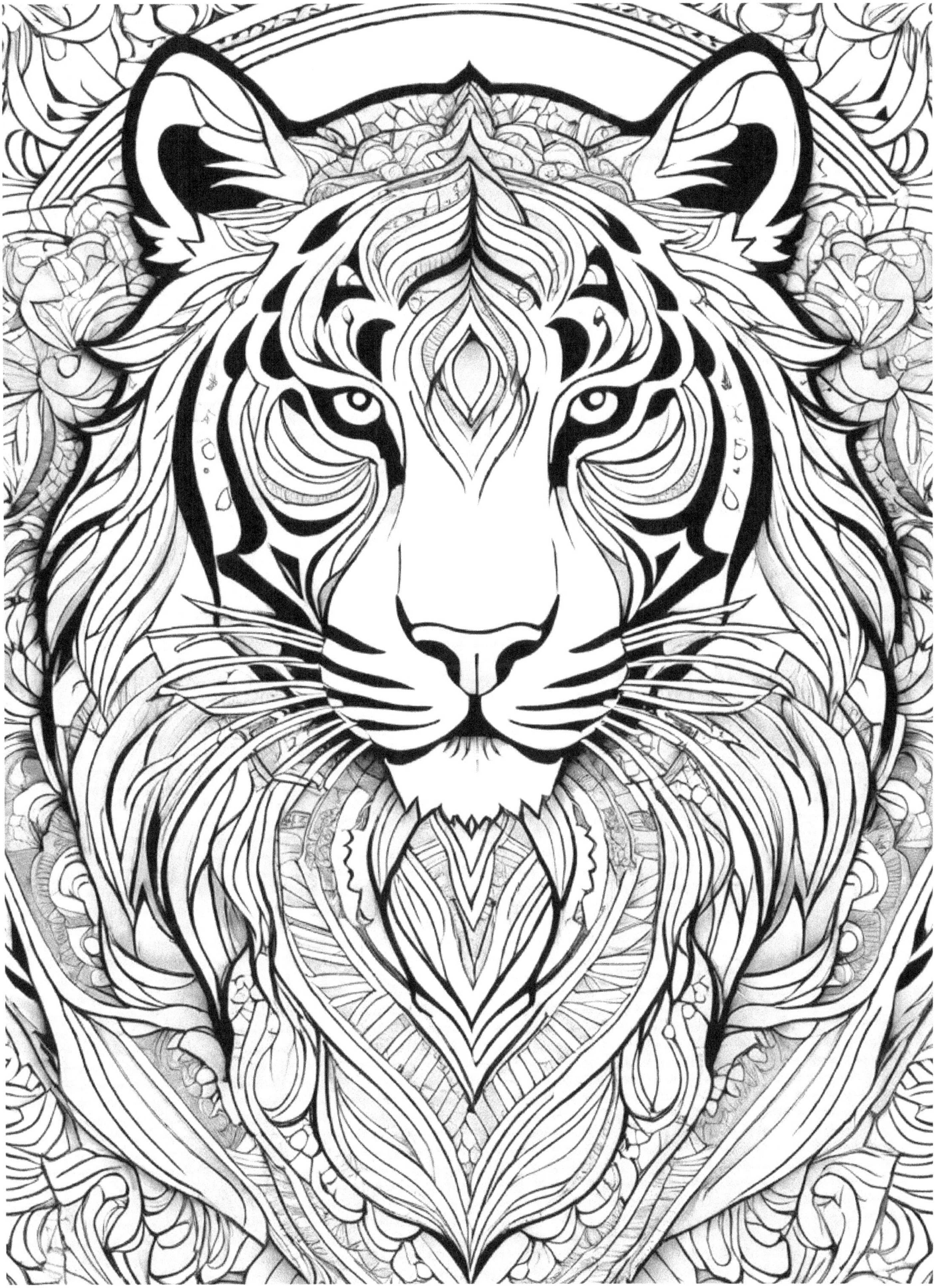

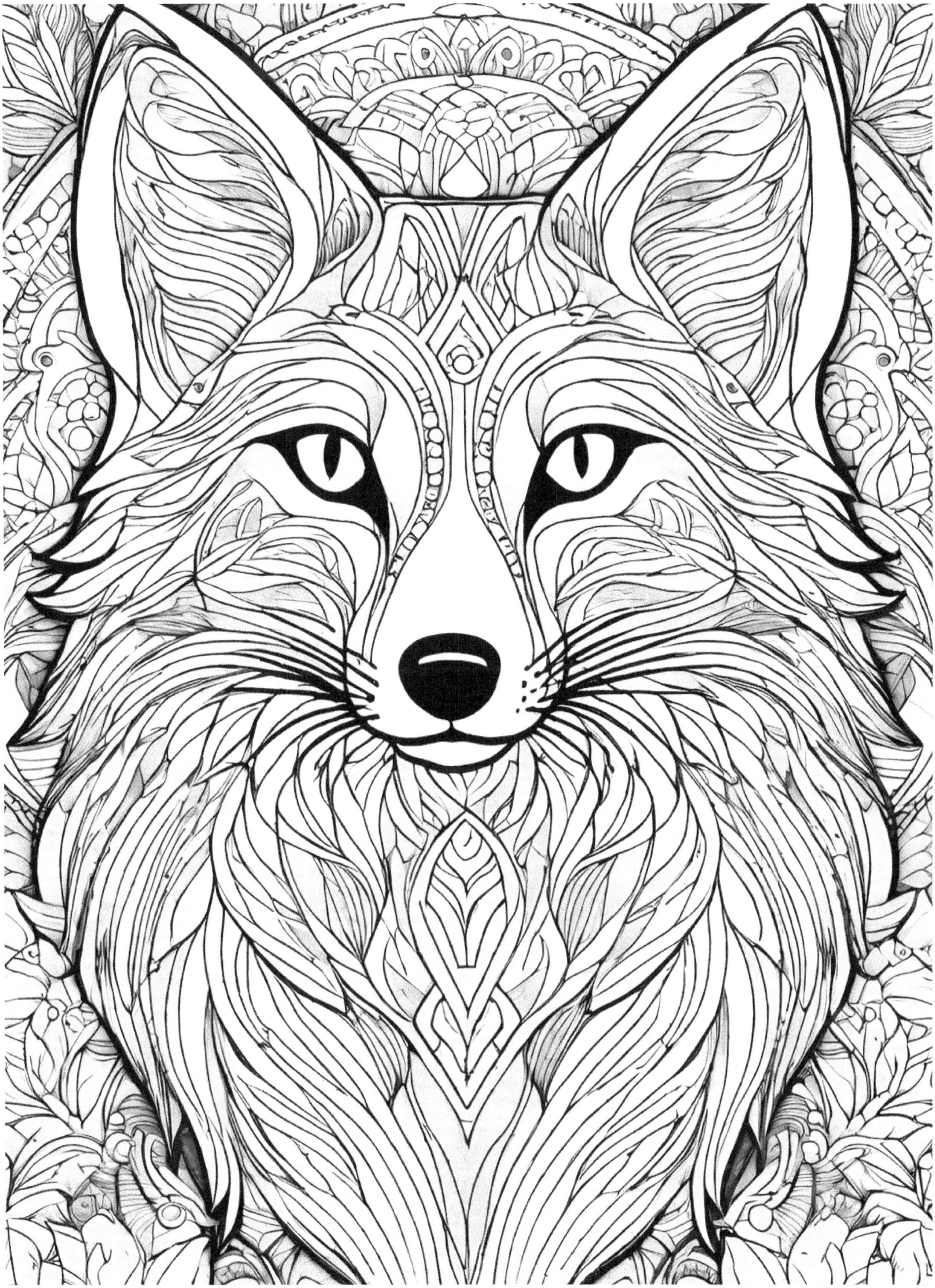

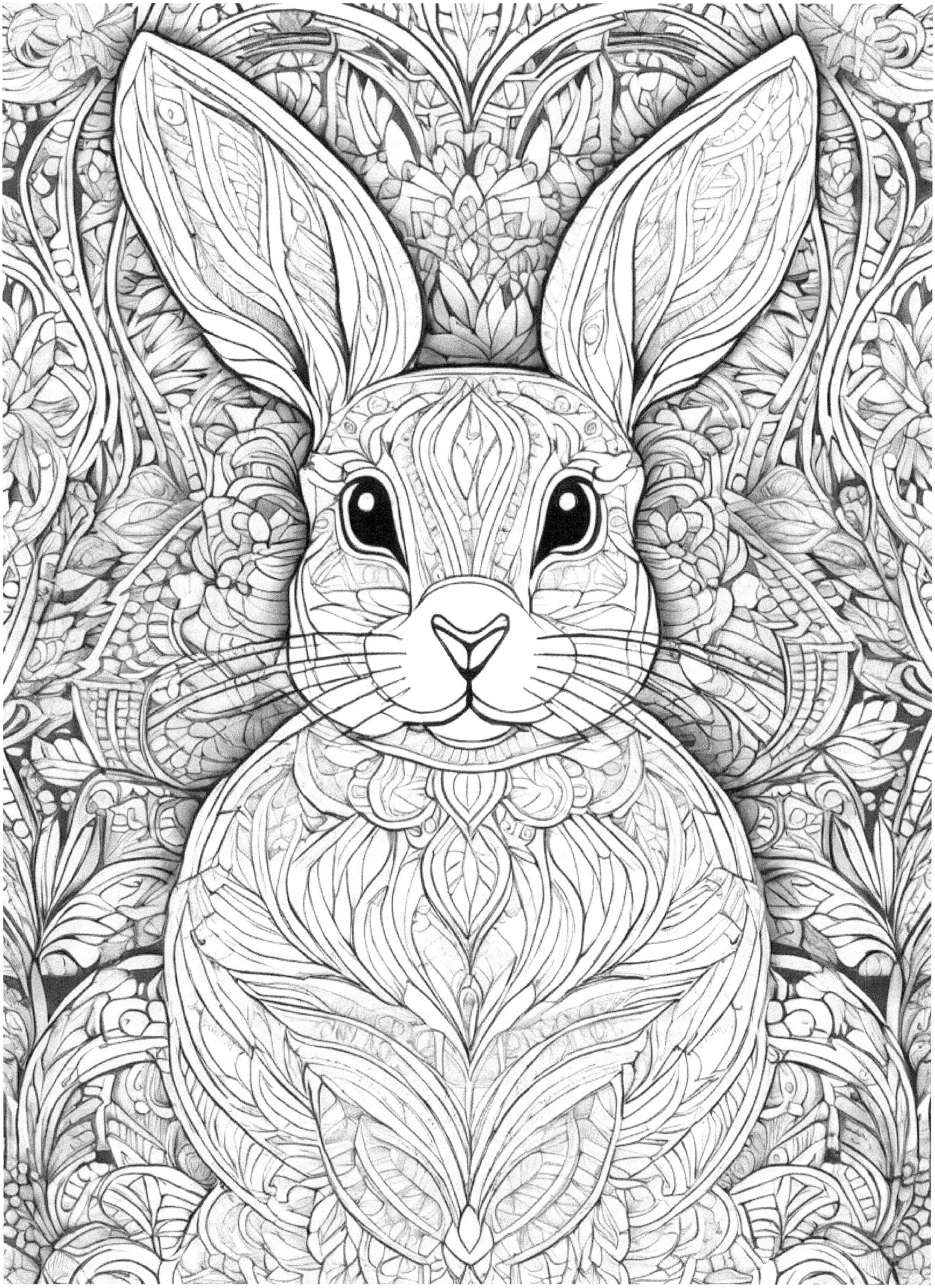

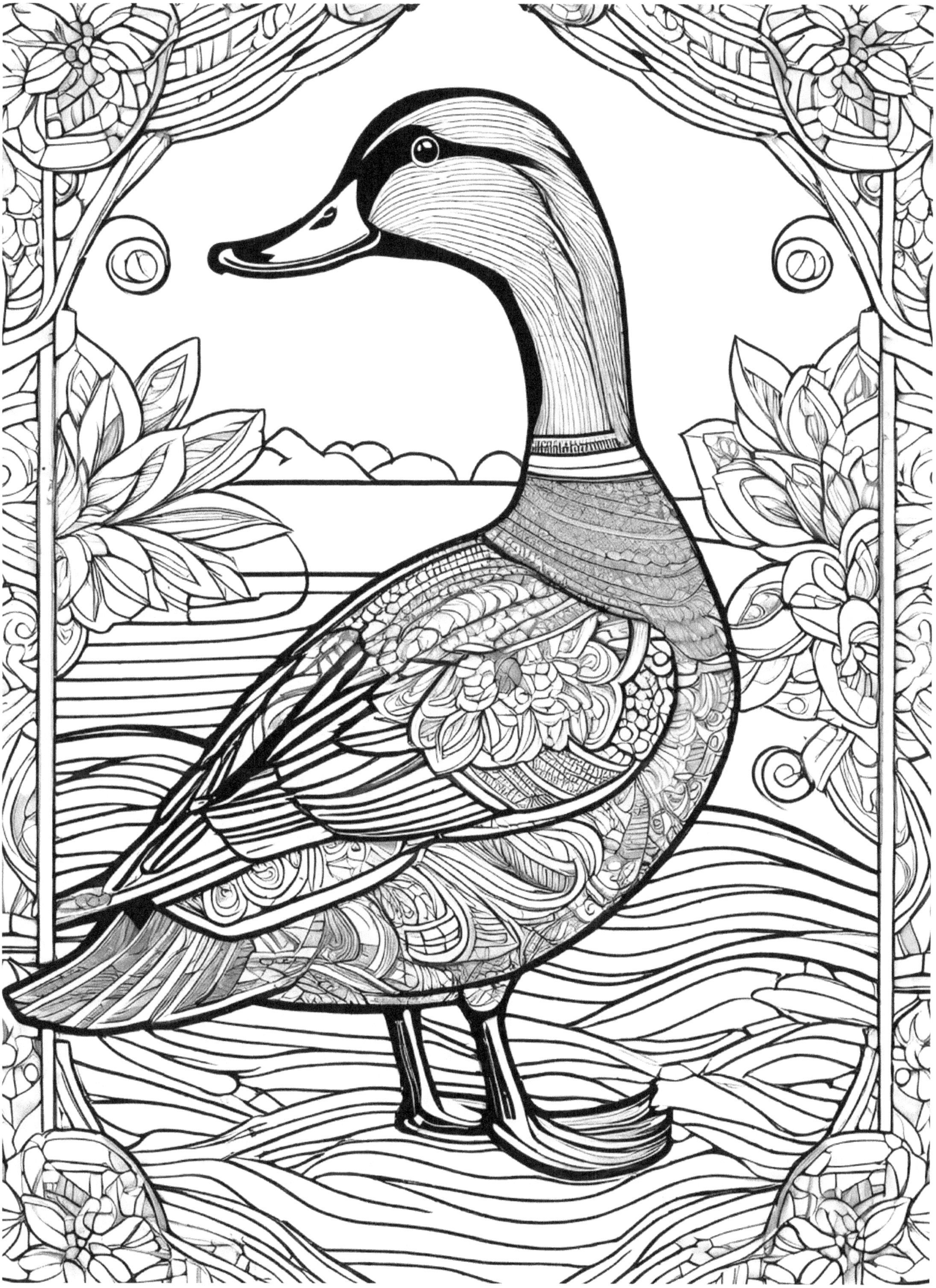

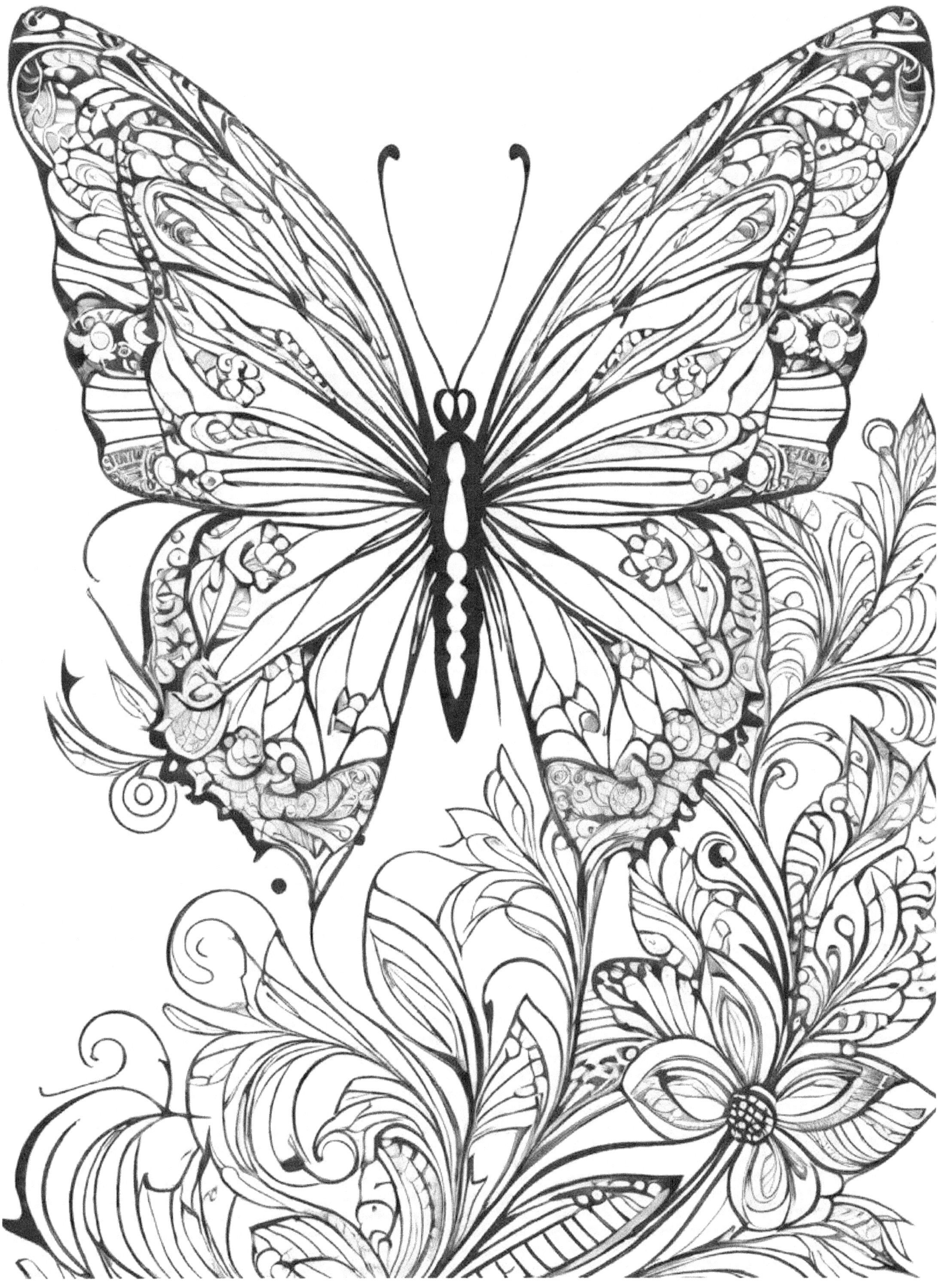

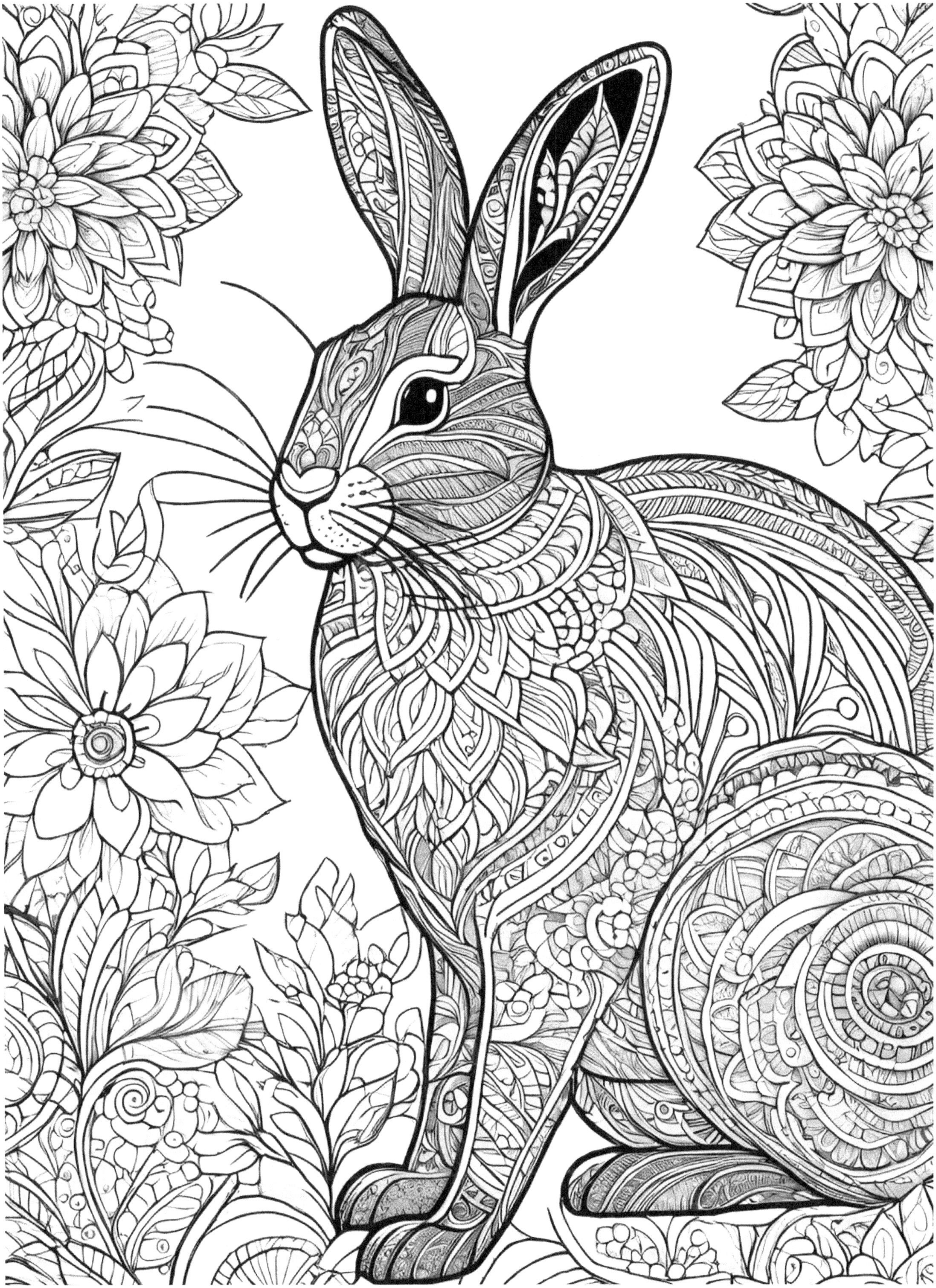

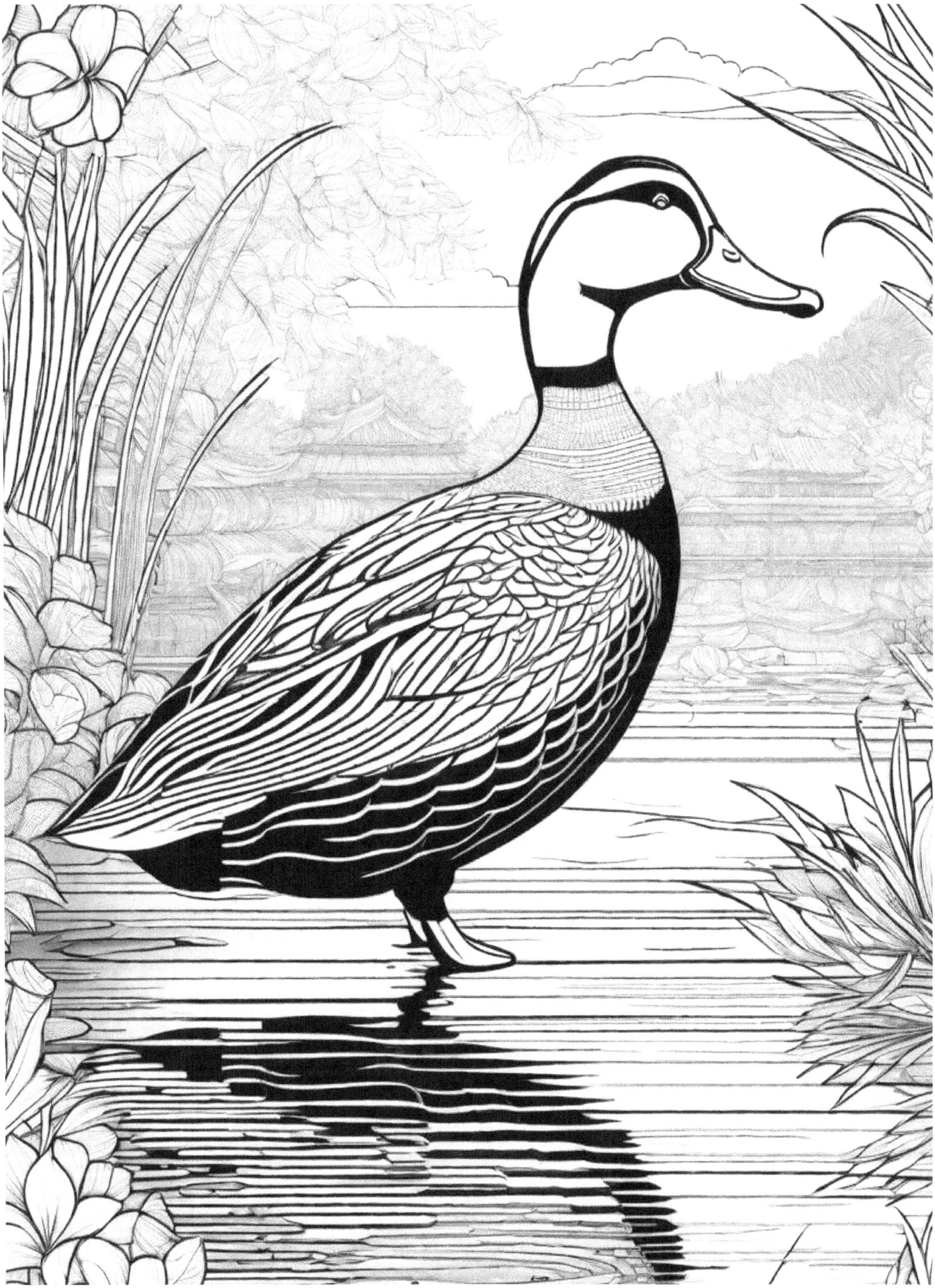

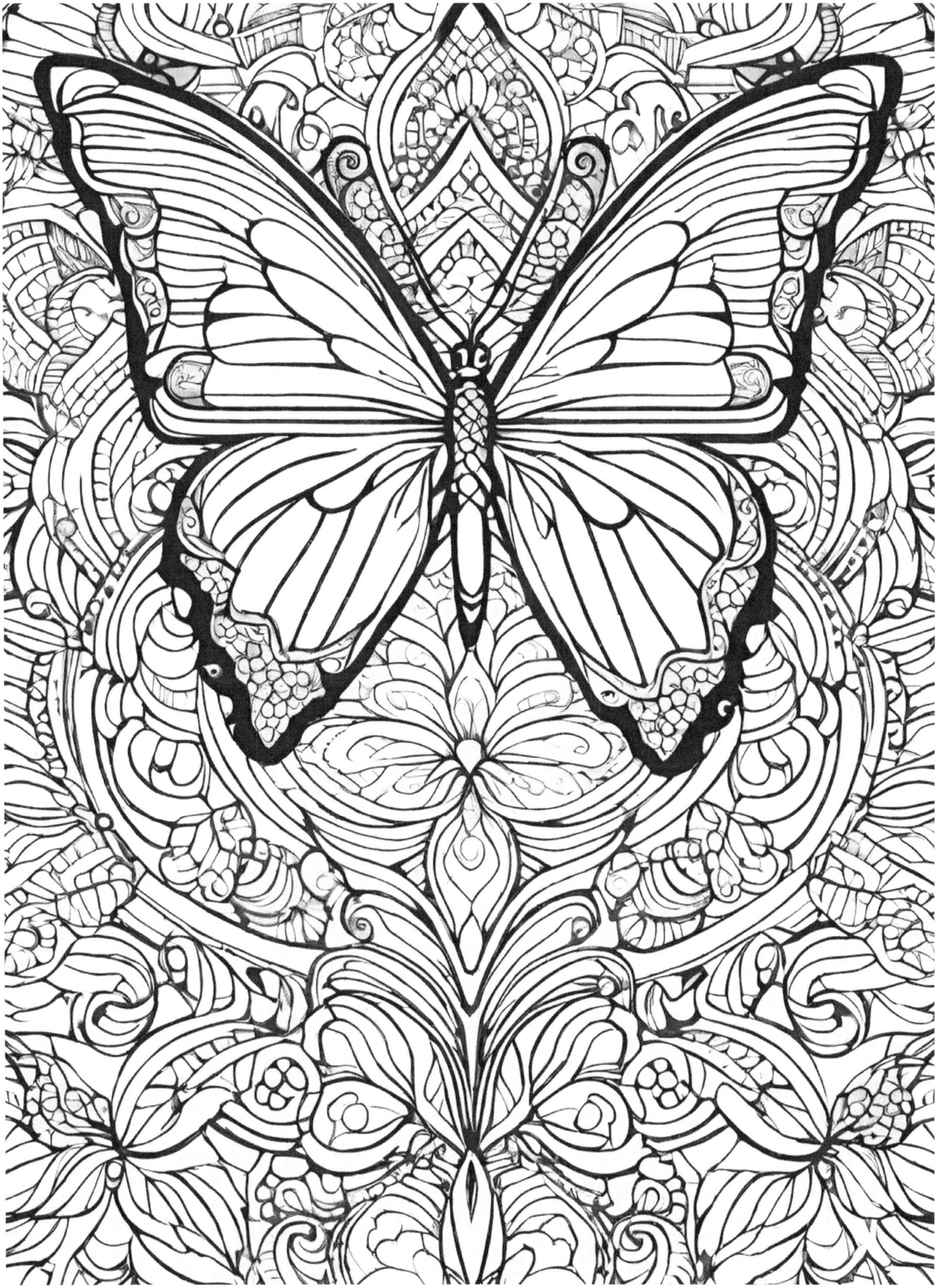

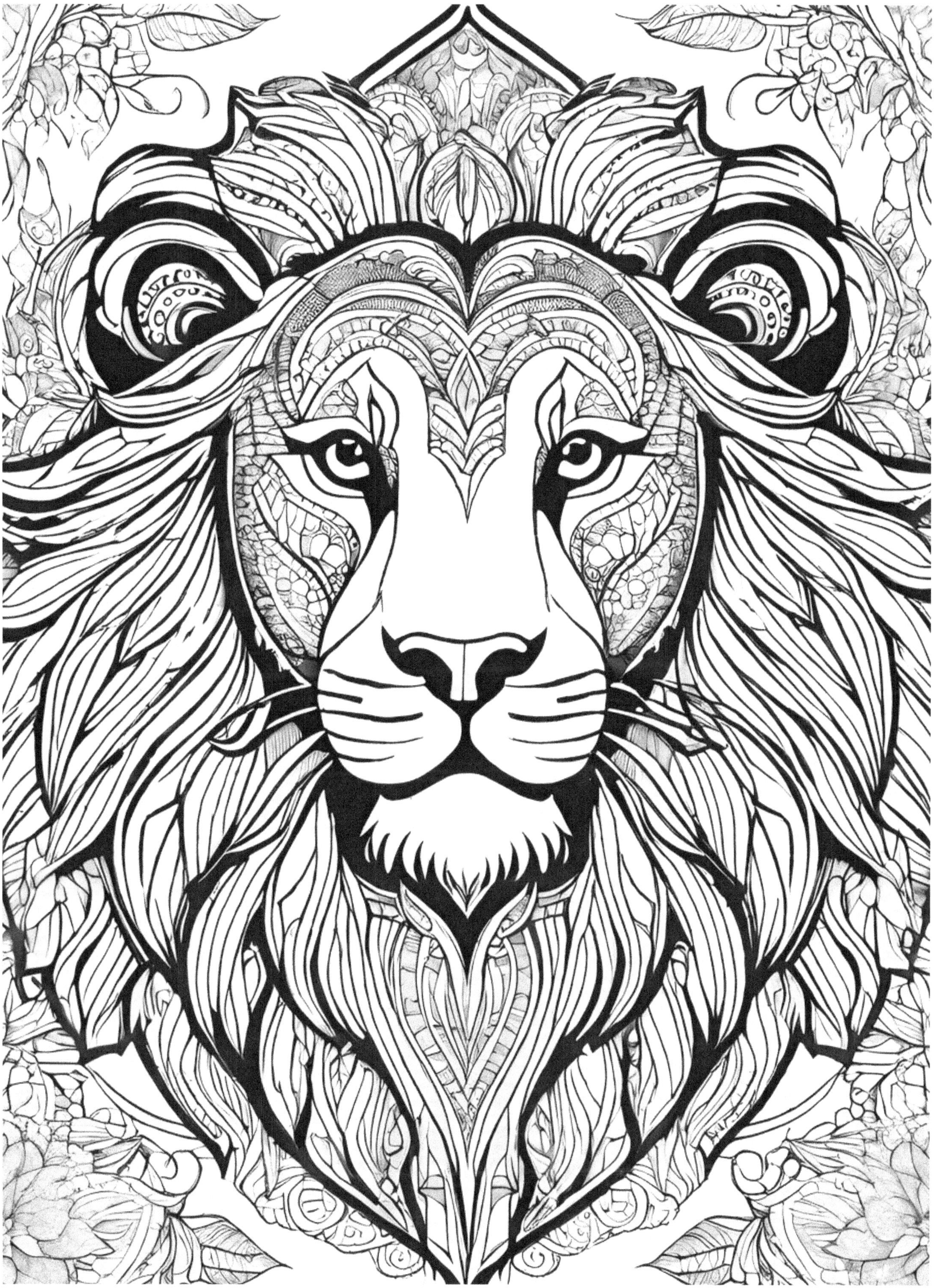

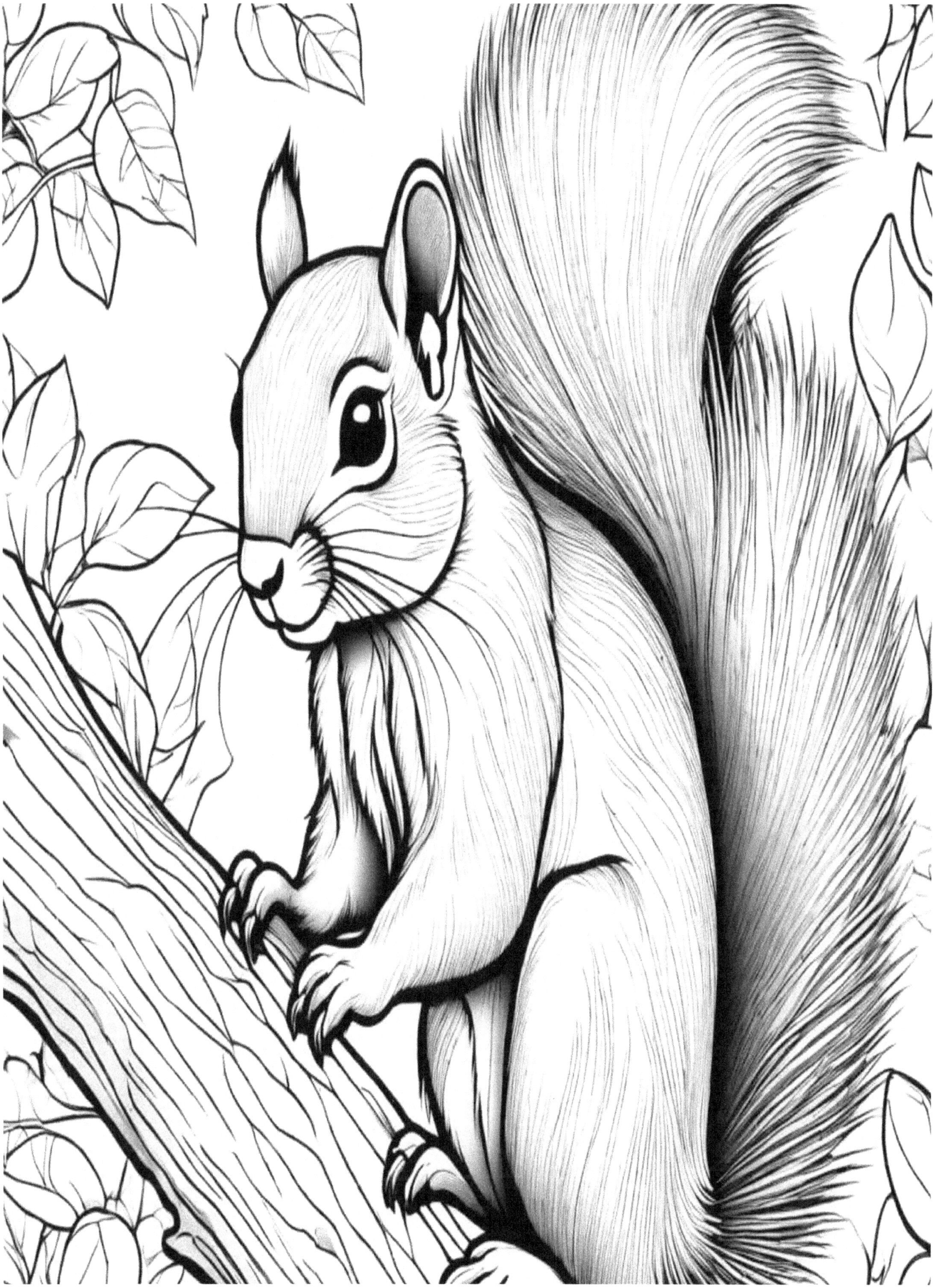

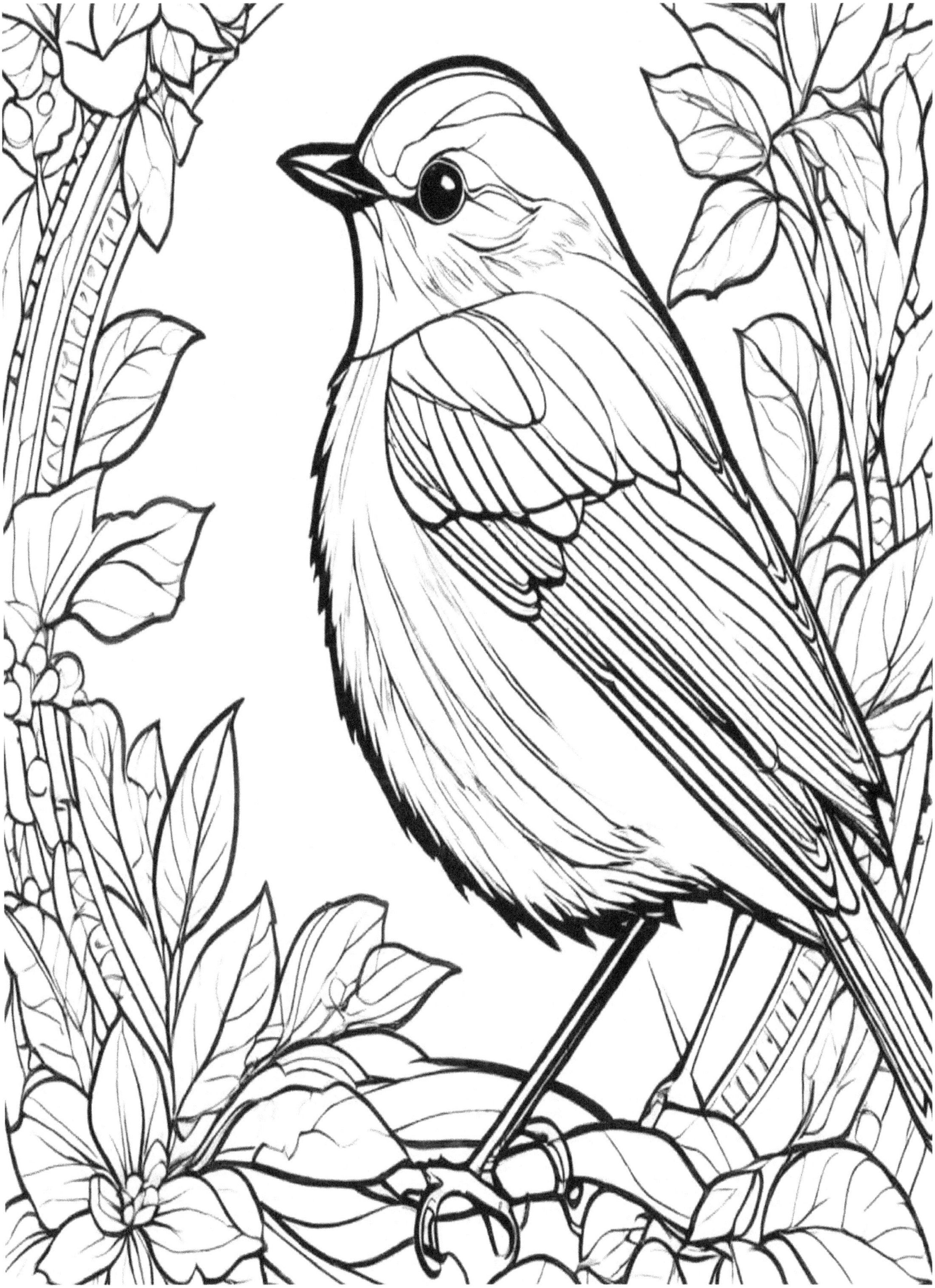

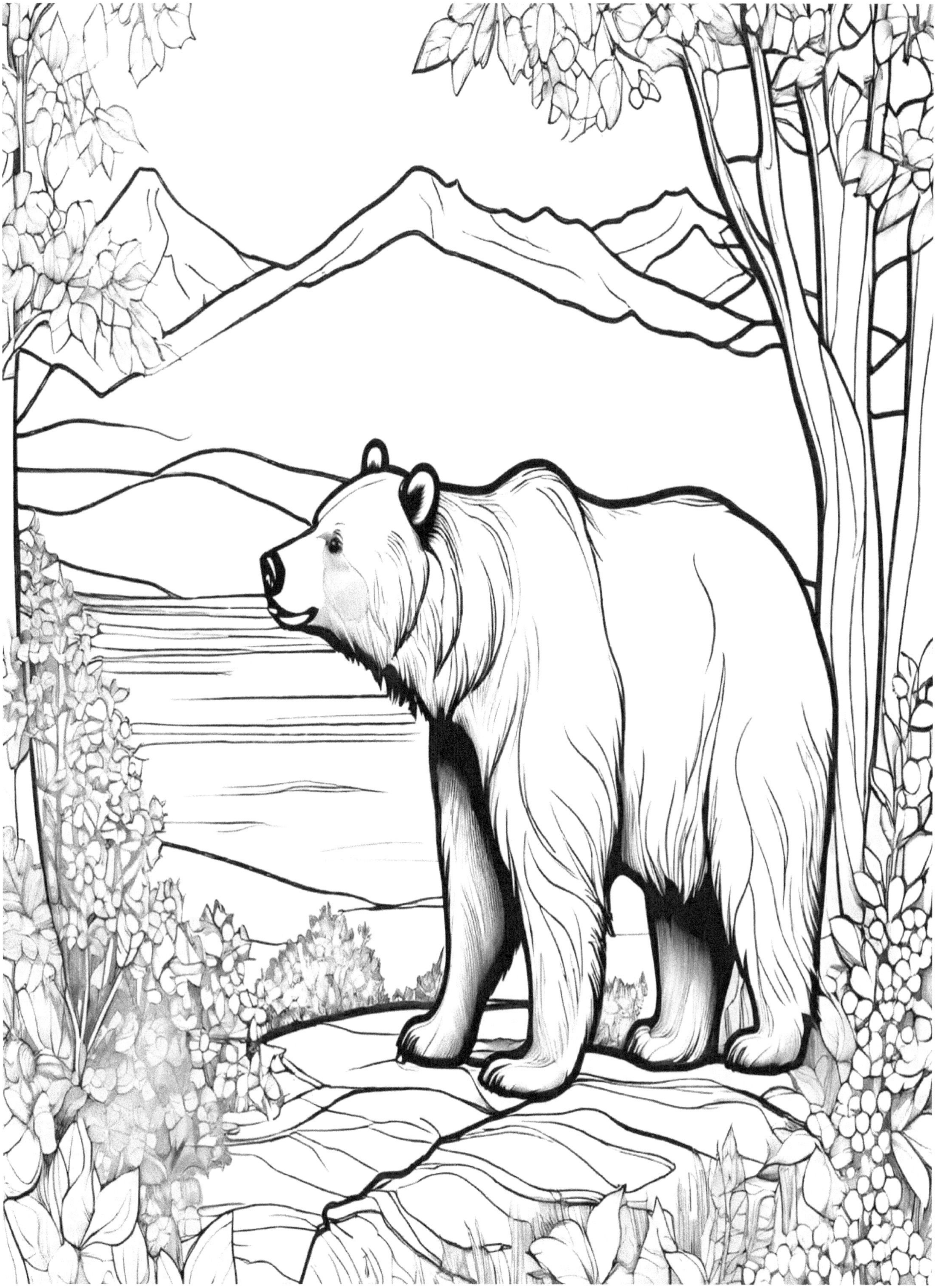

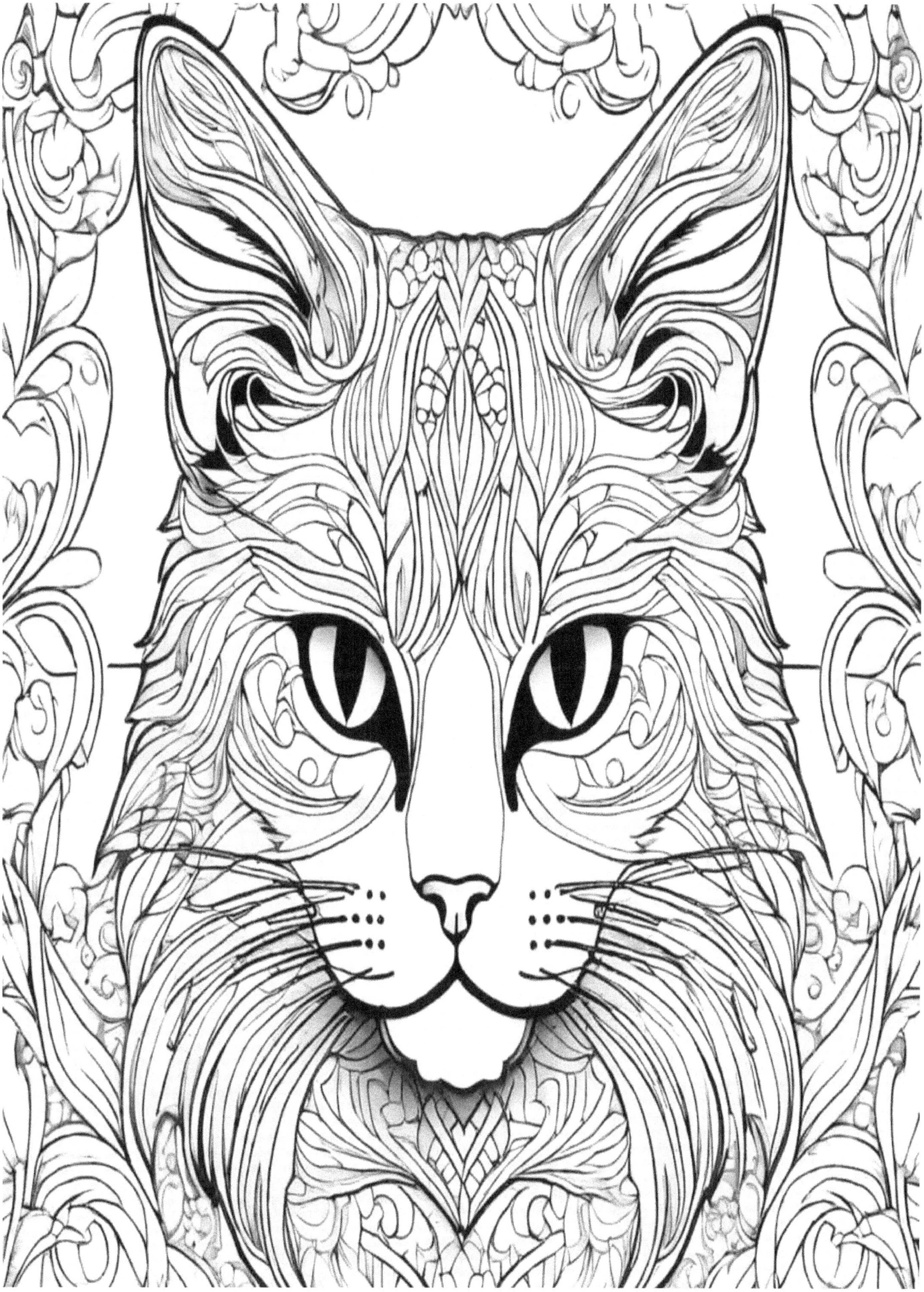

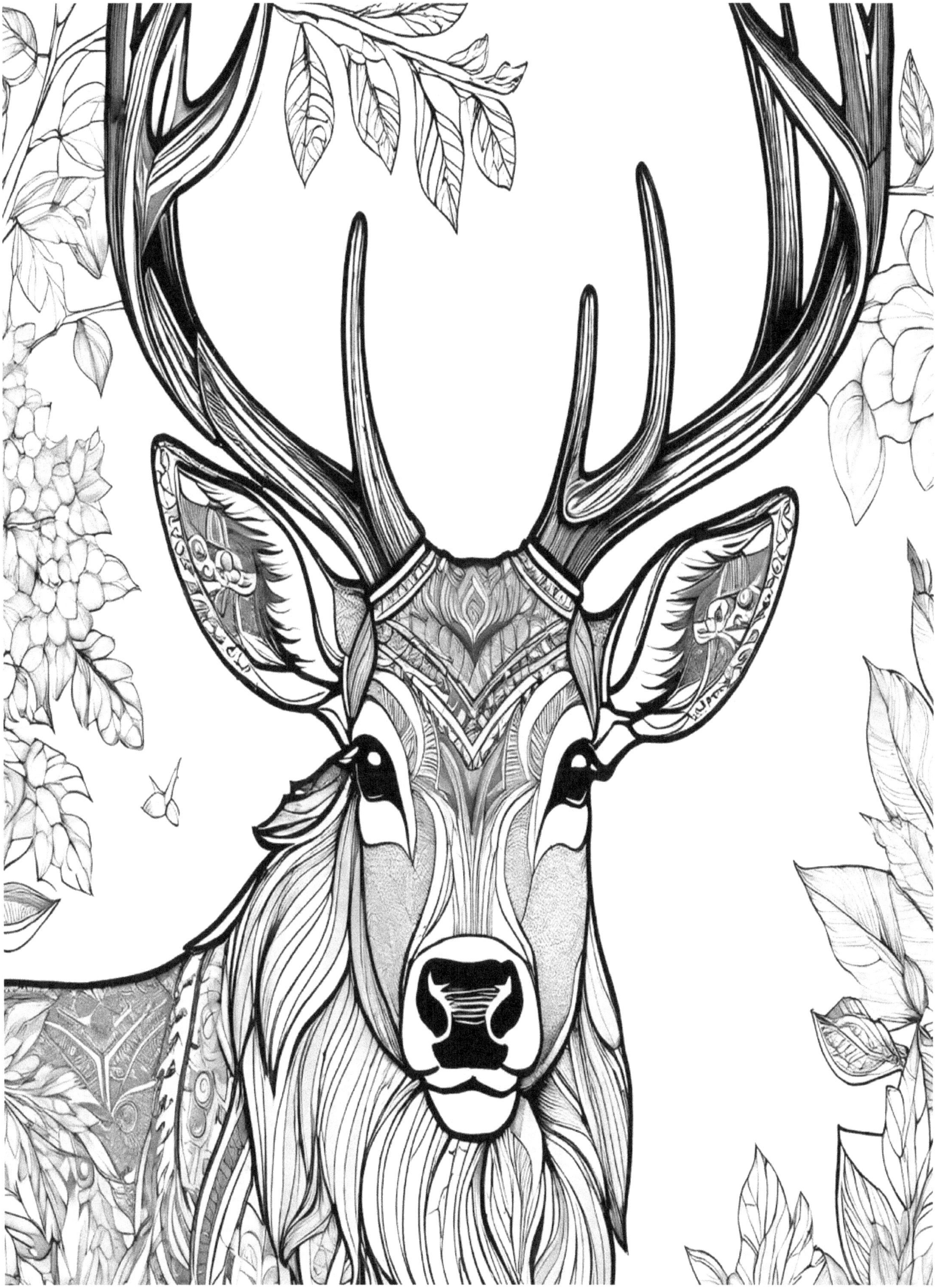

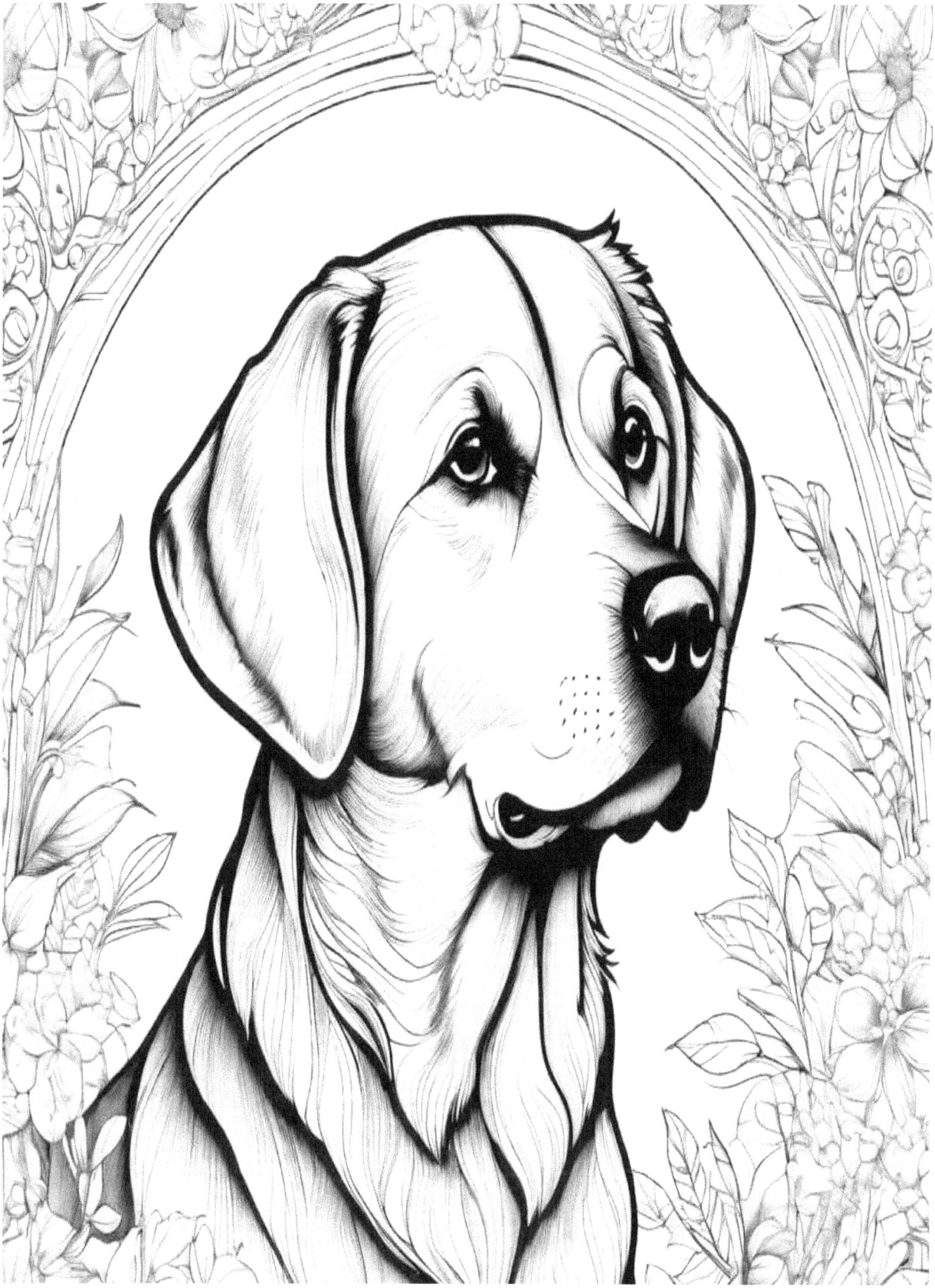

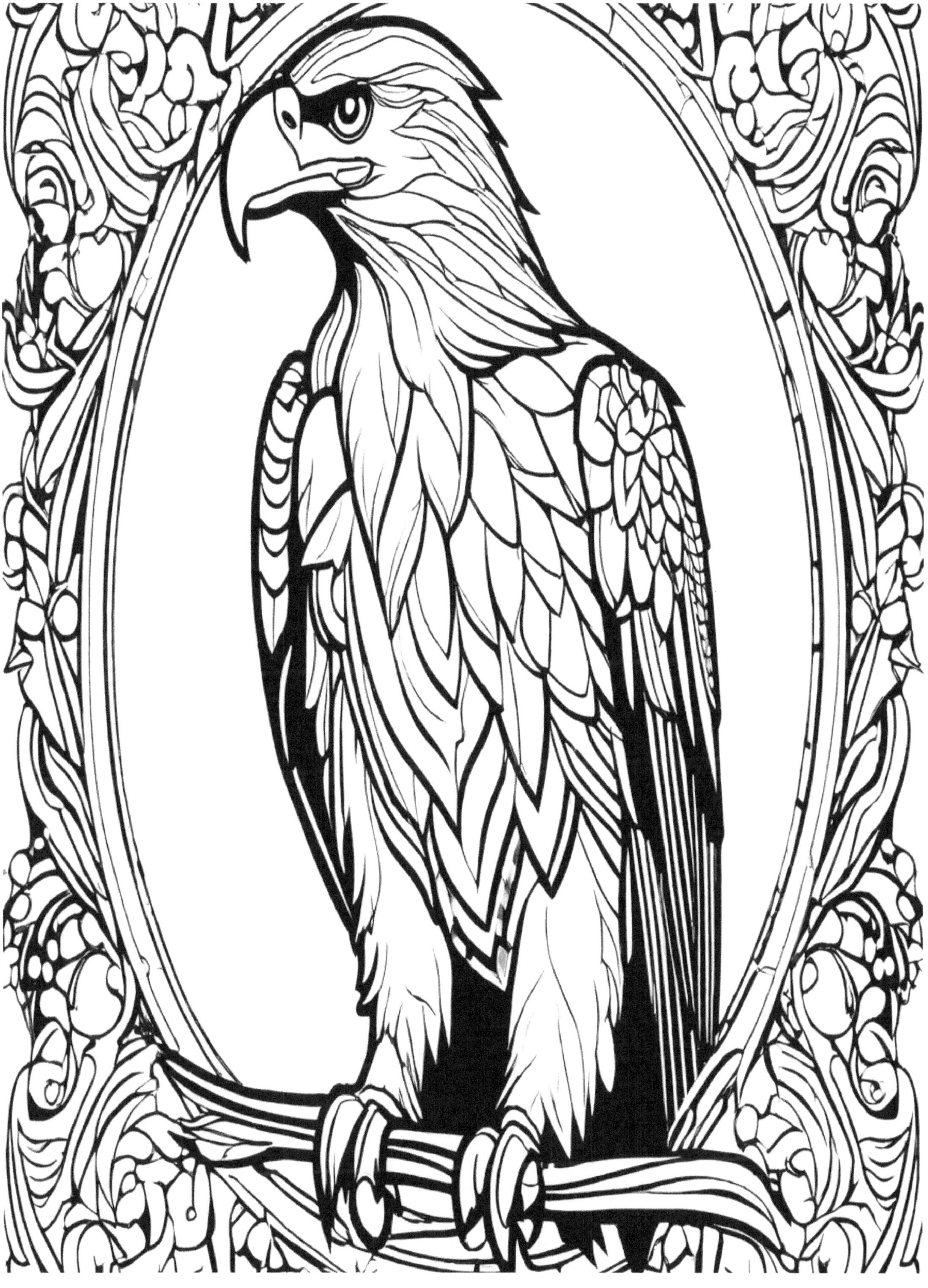

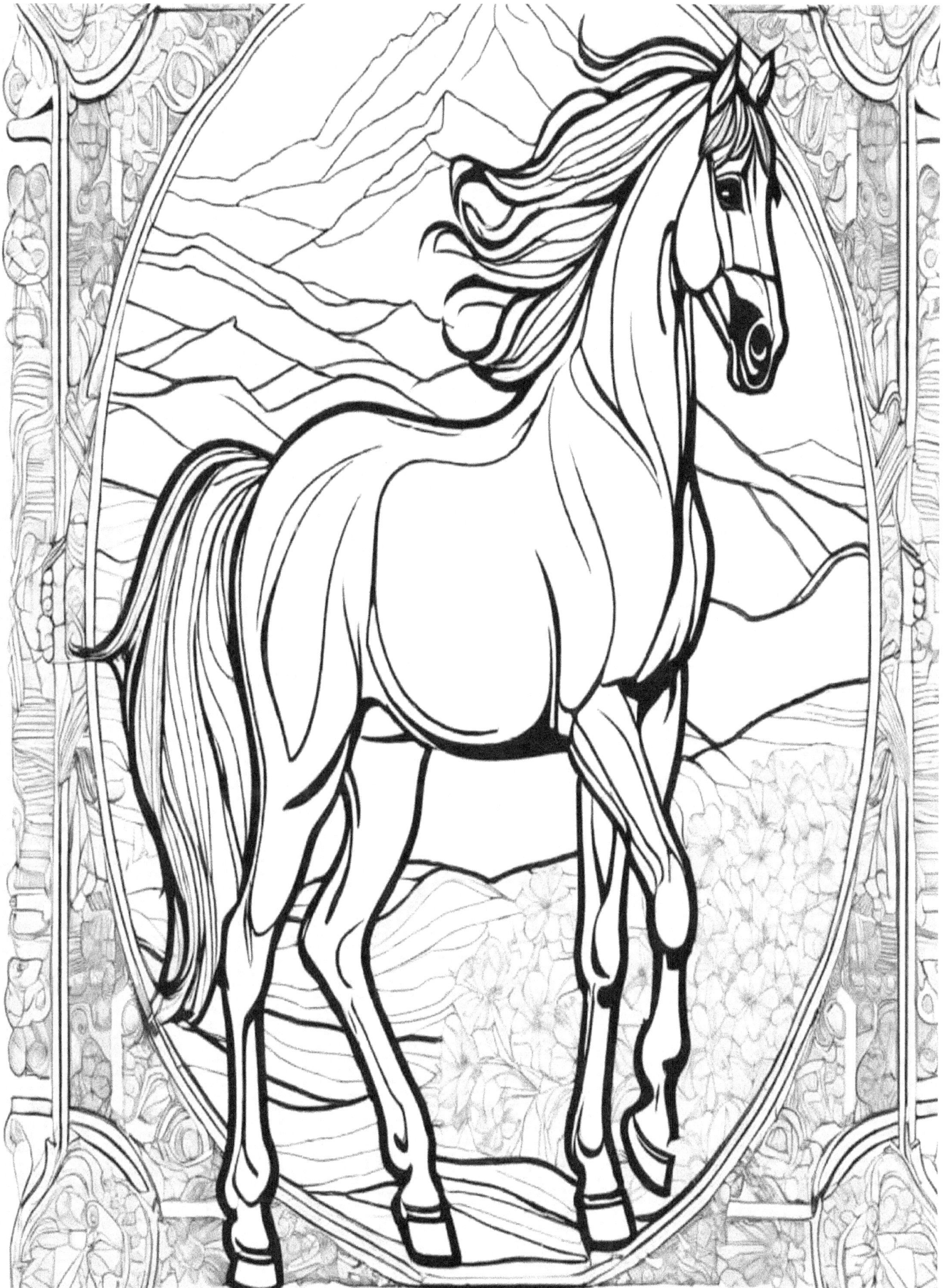

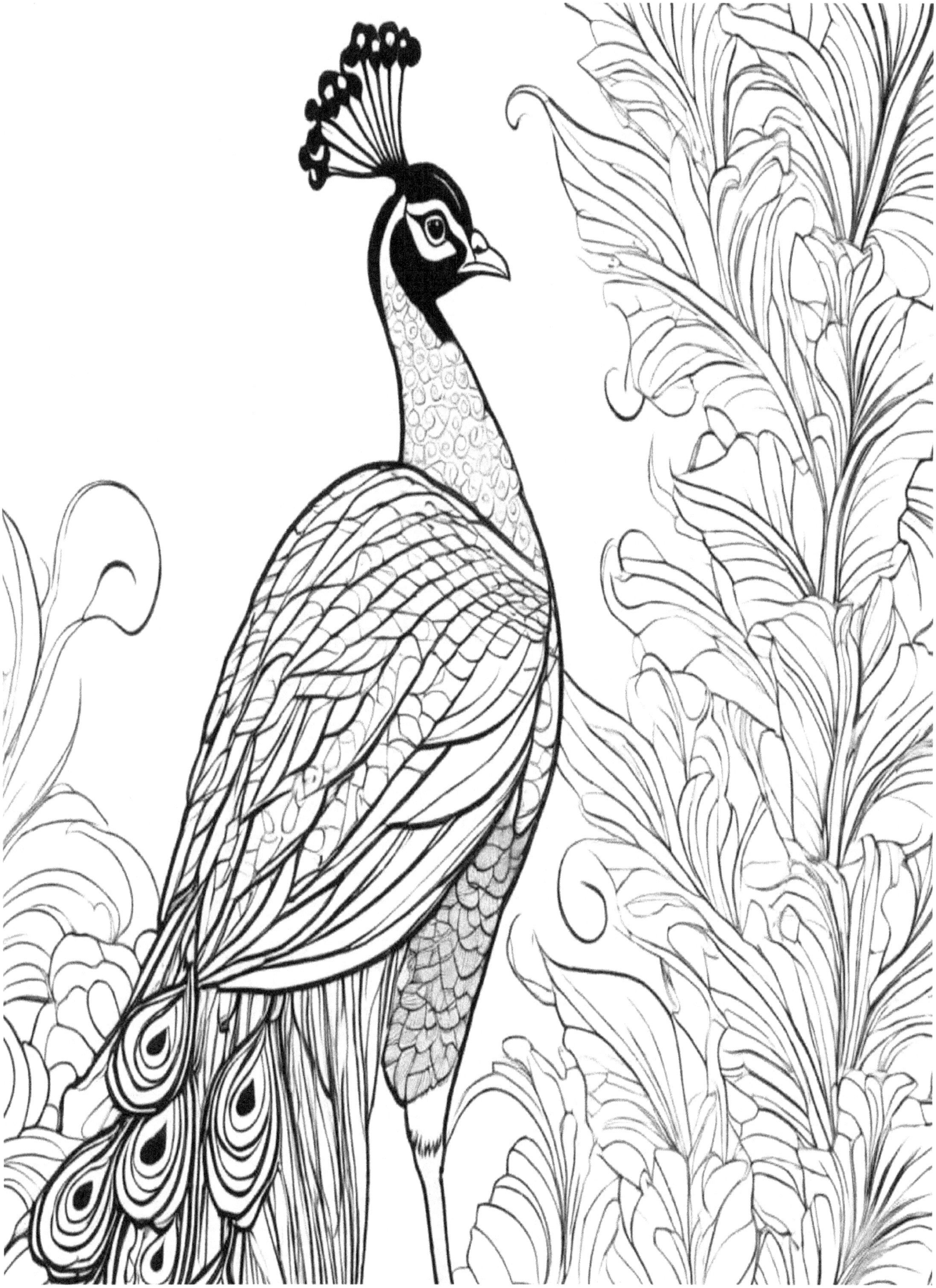

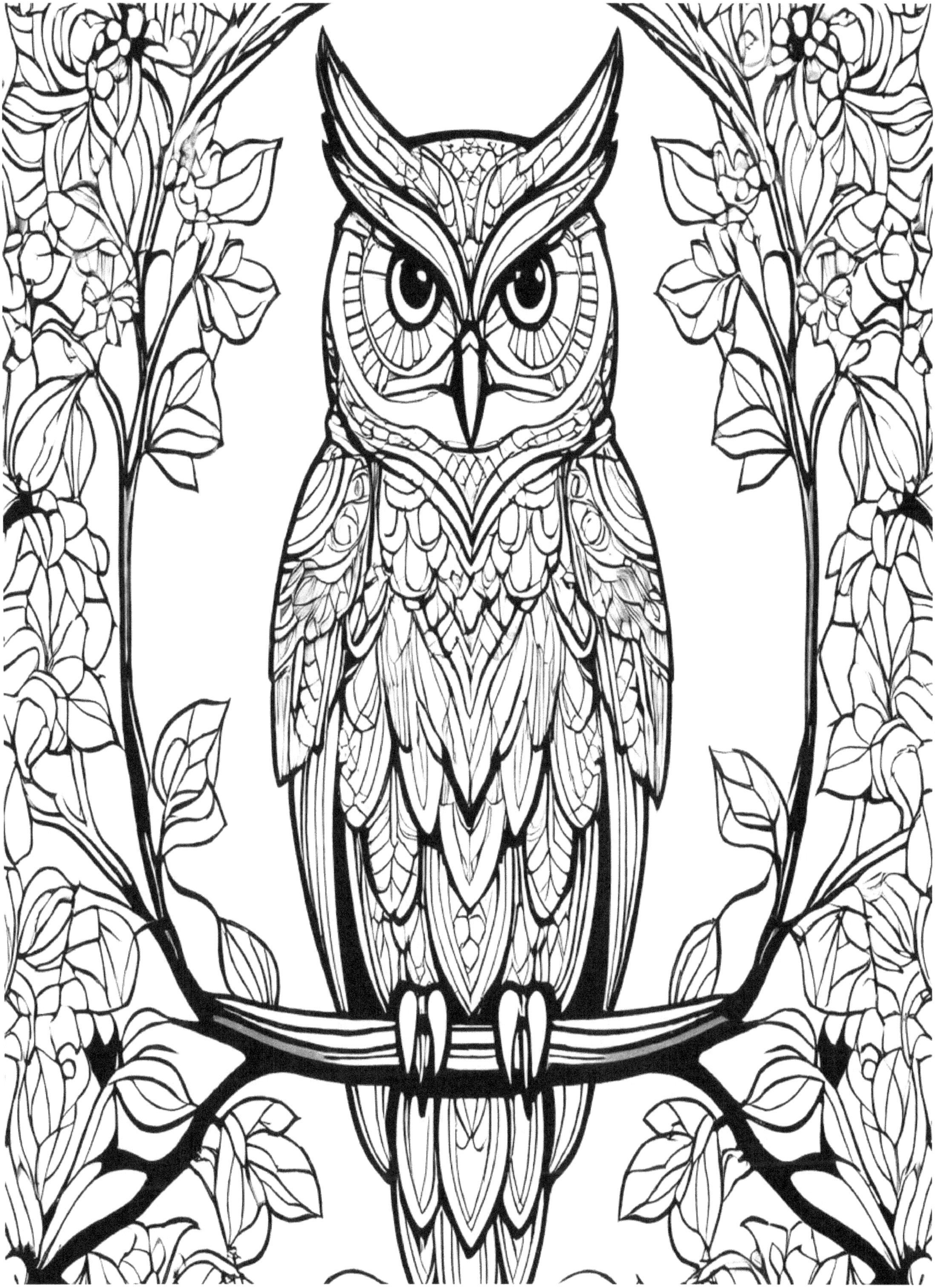

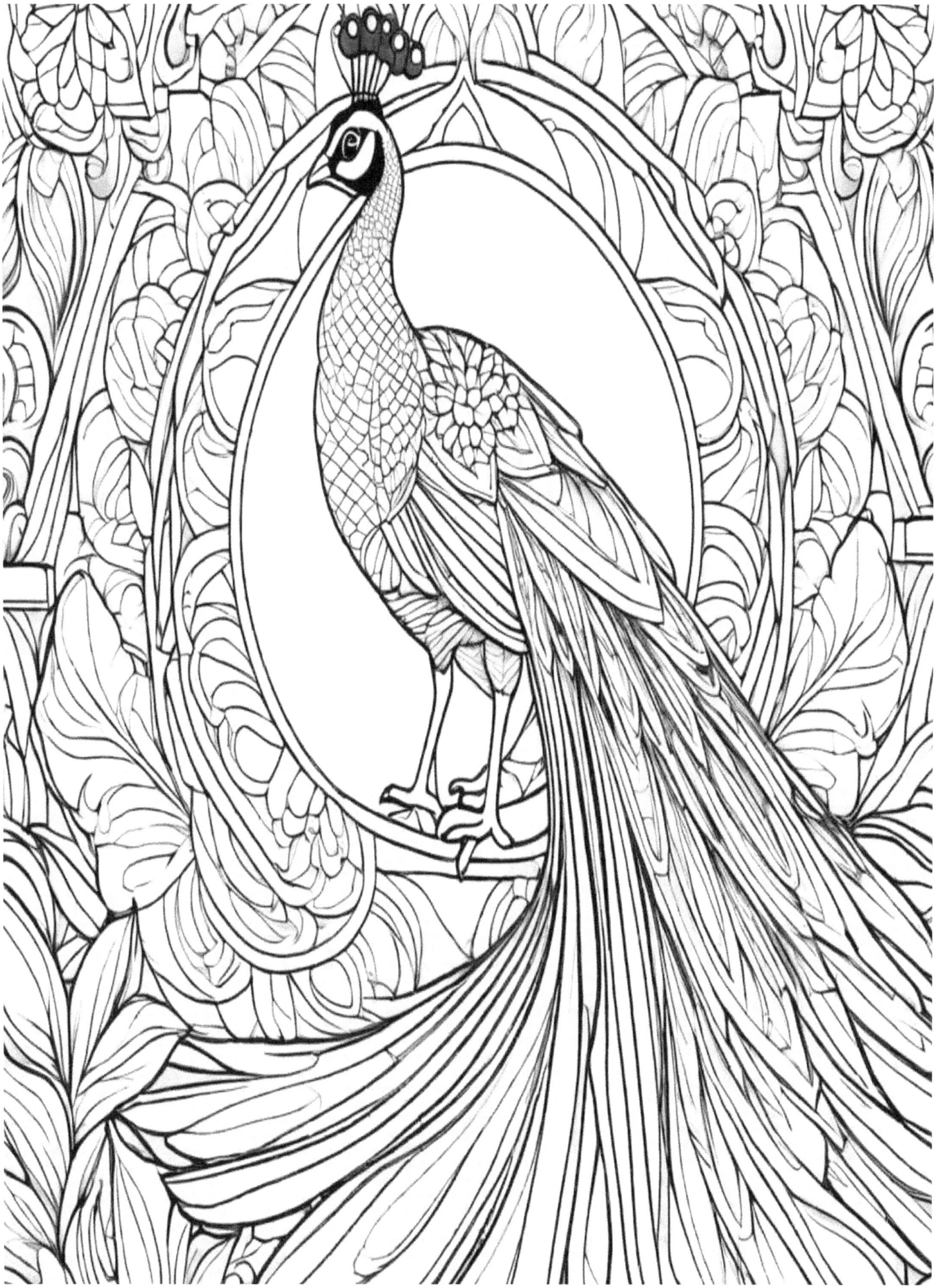

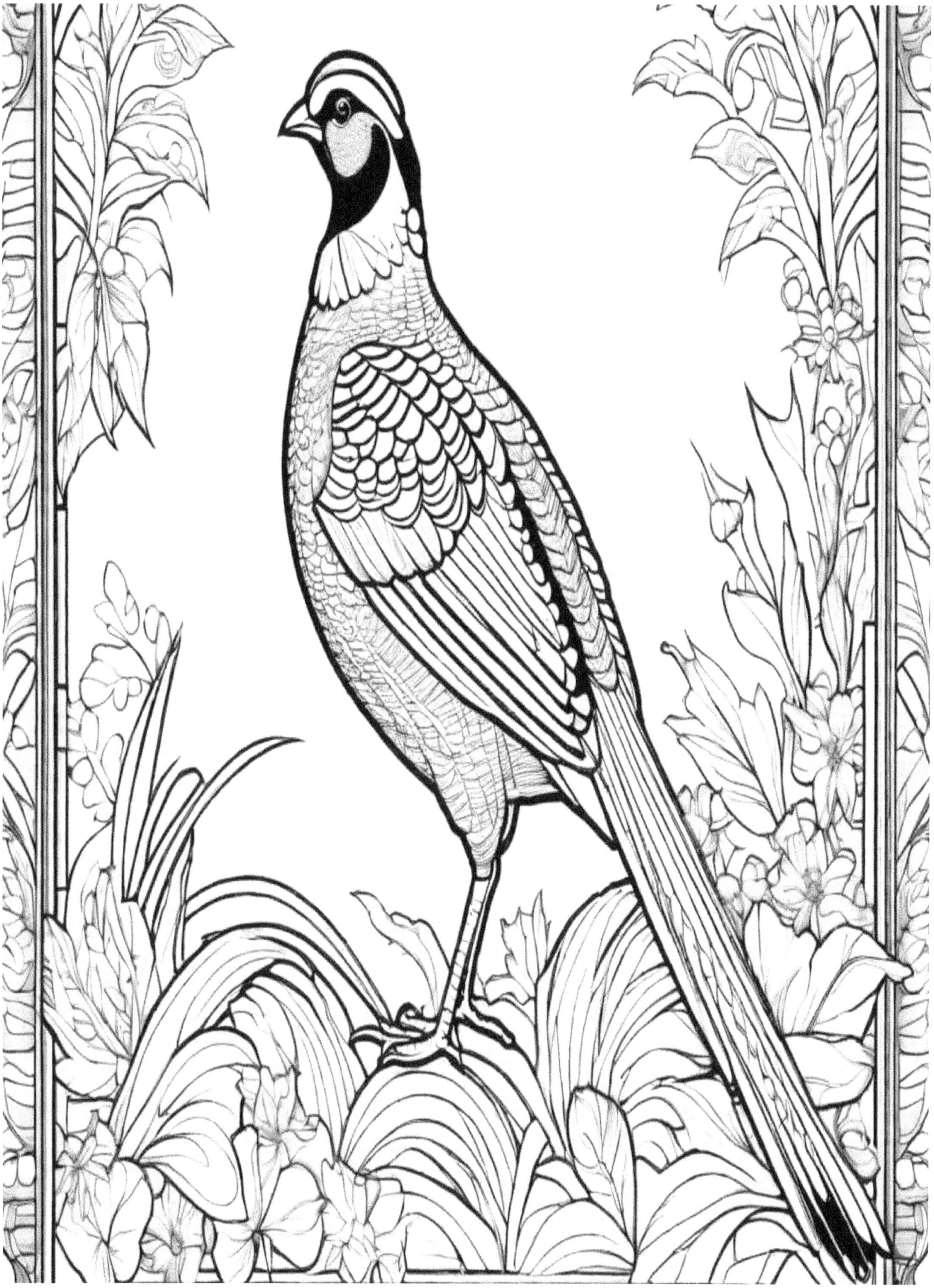

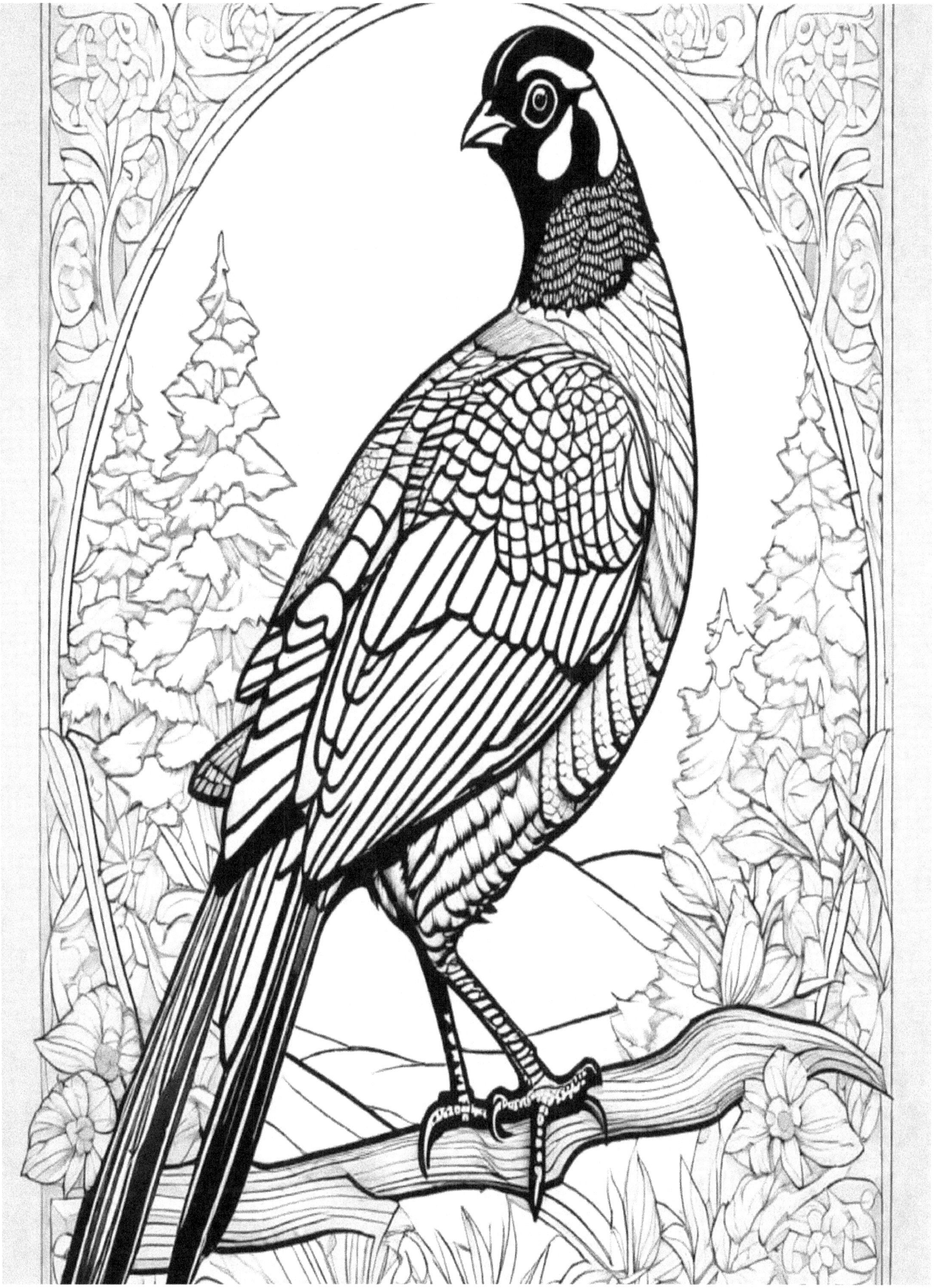

www.ingramcontent.com/pod-product-compliance
Lightning Source LLC
Chambersburg PA
CBHW082229290526
45794CB00009B/3733
9798871624432